SPACE-TACULAR

BY ALLYSON KULAVIS

downtown bookworks

downtown bookworks

Designed by Georgia Rucker
Typeset in Bryant Pro and Warugaki

PHOTO CREDITS 1: NASA (International Space Station); NASA-JPL (Venus). 2–3: NASA. 4: NASA (sun, moon surface); NASA/JPL/Cornell University (rover); Lightspring/Shutterstock.com (Earth). 5: NASA (astronaut with floating food, space shuttle, astronaut in spacesuit); NASA, ESA, HEIC, and the Hubble Heritage Team (nebula). 6: NASA/ESA. 6–7: Anastasiya Igolkina/Shutterstock.com. 7: NASA/SDO (solar flares); ©iStockphoto.com/Joel Carillet (sunburn). 8: NASA/JPL. 9: NASA/JPL (Great Red Spot); NASA/JPL/Space Science Institute (Jupiter). 10: NASA/JPL. 11: NASA/JPL, Magellan Team (arachnoids); Terrence Emerson/Shutterstock.com (night sky); NASA-JPL (Venus). 12: NASA (far side of the moon); ©Exactostock/SuperStock (moon surface). 13: NASA (all). 14: NASA/ESA. 15: NASA/JPL-Caltech/STScI/ Vassar (glowing eyes galaxies); NASA, ESA, and the Hubble Heritage Team (Antennae Galaxies); NASA, J. Englsih, U. Manitoba, S. Hunsberger, S. Zonak, J. Charlton, S. Gallagher and L. Frattare (four galaxies). 16: NASA, ESA, K. Noll (Bow Tie Nebula); NASA/Andrew Fruchter (Eskimo Nebula); NASA, ESA, M. Livio and the Hubble 20th anniversary team (stars being born). 17: NASA, ESA, J. Hester, A. Loll. 18: NASA-JPL (all). 19: ©age fotostock/SuperStock. 20: ©Eye Ubiquitous/SuperStock. 20–21 ©Science Faction/SuperStock. 21: NASA. 22: NASA/JHUAPL (Eros); NASA/JPL (Ida). 23: Walter G. Arce/Shutterstock.com (crater from above); markrhiggins/Shutterstock.com (crater from rim). 24: NASA/VAFB. 25: NASA (both). 26: NASA/ STScI. 27: NASA (both). 28: NASA and the Hubble Heritage Team. 29: NASA, ESA, and the Hubble Heritage Team (rose-shaped galaxy); NASA, ESA, C.R. O'Dell, M. Meixner, P. McCullough (nebula); NASA, ESA, STSci, J. Hester, and P. Scowen (gas columns). 30: AP Photo/NASA. 31: Mark Kauffman/Time and Life Pictures/ Getty Images (Sputnik 5); NASA (astronaut with newt). 32–41: NASA (all). 42: NASA/JPL/Cornell University. 43: NASA/JPL (both). 44–45: NASA. 46: maniacpixel/Shutterstock.com (golf ball); Jiri Hera/Shutterstock. com (baby food); Maxim Godkin/Shutterstock.com (glasses). 47: NASA/JPL-Caltech (scientists); Ruslan Kudrin/Shutterstock.com (swimsuit); NASA (bootprint). 48: NASA/Ames Research Center (scientist with tektites); Ken Pilon/BigStockPhoto.com (tektites).

Printed in China, October 2011

ISBN 9781935703488

10 9 8 7 6 5 4 3 2 1

Downtown Bookworks Inc.
285 West Broadway
New York, NY 10013

www.downtownbookworks.com

CONTENTS

OUT OF THIS WORLD!

Space is filled with countless mind-blowing and mysterious things. In these pages, you will read about stars and satellites, comets and cannibal galaxies, asteroids and astronauts. You can take a closer look at a few of the planets in our solar system, see amazing photos of deep space, and get a glimpse into daily life aboard the International Space Station. You may even find out if space travel is in your future.

- What does it feel like to leave Earth's atmosphere?
- Why do some stars seem to be blinking in the night sky?
- How do robots get around on Mars?
- Can astronauts have candy in space?

For answers to these questions and more, read on.

OUR STAR: THE SUN

The sun is the star at the center of our solar system. Earth orbits around the sun.

Unlike planets and moons, stars have no solid core. Instead, they are made entirely of exploding gases. Stars can glow in a variety of colors. Brown stars are the coolest, and blue are the hottest. Our sun is a medium-sized, yellow star. It's actually pretty average. Many stars are larger and hotter than our sun.

This shot was taken with a special camera that shows the different temperatures on the outer layer of the sun. The red areas are about 3.6 million degrees Fahrenheit. The "cooler" blue areas are about 1.8 million degrees.

The sun is the only star we can study up close, but the light is so bright that we have to use special cameras and filters to see what's happening on the surface. The light we see was actually created in the sun's core 10,000 to 170,000 years ago. It takes that long for light energy to make its way through the many layers of the sun's gases.

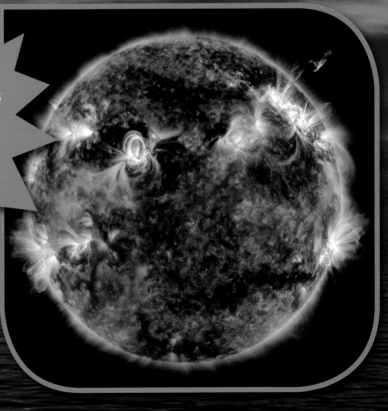

The solar flares seen in this photo are the result of enormous explosions. The sun's gravity then pulls the explosions back toward its center, creating the fiery loops you see here.

The light energy from the sun is so powerful that it can burn your skin after traveling 93 million miles through space.

A GIANT AMONG GIANTS: JUPITER

Jupiter is by far the largest planet that orbits the sun. It's two and a half times larger than Mercury, Venus, Earth, Mars, Saturn, Uranus, and Neptune put together.

Jupiter is called a gas giant because most of the planet is made of liquid and gas. It has a stormy atmosphere with winds of almost 400 miles per hour and lightning 1,000 times more powerful than the lightning on Earth.

The magnetic fields around Jupiter are about 20 times larger than the sun and reach past Saturn. There's so much radiation in these invisible fields that it would kill anyone trying to pass through them.

NASA scientists created this collage of Jupiter and some of its huge moons.

Jupiter

Io

Europa

Ganymede is the largest moon in our solar system.

About 1,400 Earths could fit inside Jupiter.

The Great Red Spot is a huge storm that's been raging for nearly 300 years! It's more than 12,000 miles across, and was almost twice as big 100 years ago.

JUPITER

VOLCANIC INFERNO: VENUS

The most hostile environment of any planet in our solar system is found on Venus.

Unlike Earth, Venus has no trees or oceans to help absorb the carbon dioxide gas its volcanoes having been burping up for billions of years. All of that extra carbon dioxide traps heat from the sun, making the surface of Venus hot enough to melt lead. It can be more than 850°F. That's really, really hot.

There are clouds of sulfuric acid on Venus that are powerful enough to corrode metal and destroy instruments on space probes. These clouds give new meaning to the term *acid rain*. The Soviet probe Venera 7 landed on Venus in 1970 and only lasted 23 minutes in the harsh environment before it kicked the bucket.

> Venus rotates on its axis in the opposite direction than the other planets in our solar system.

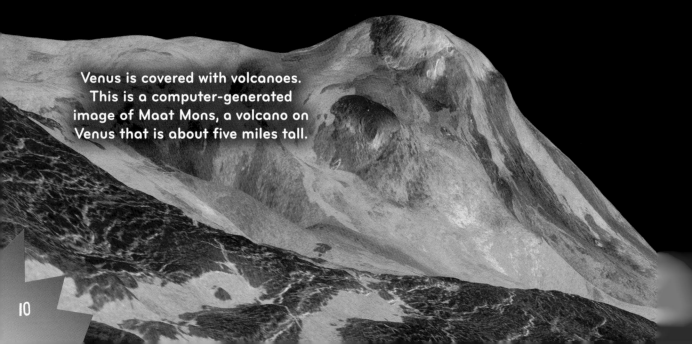

Venus is covered with volcanoes. This is a computer-generated image of Maat Mons, a volcano on Venus that is about five miles tall.

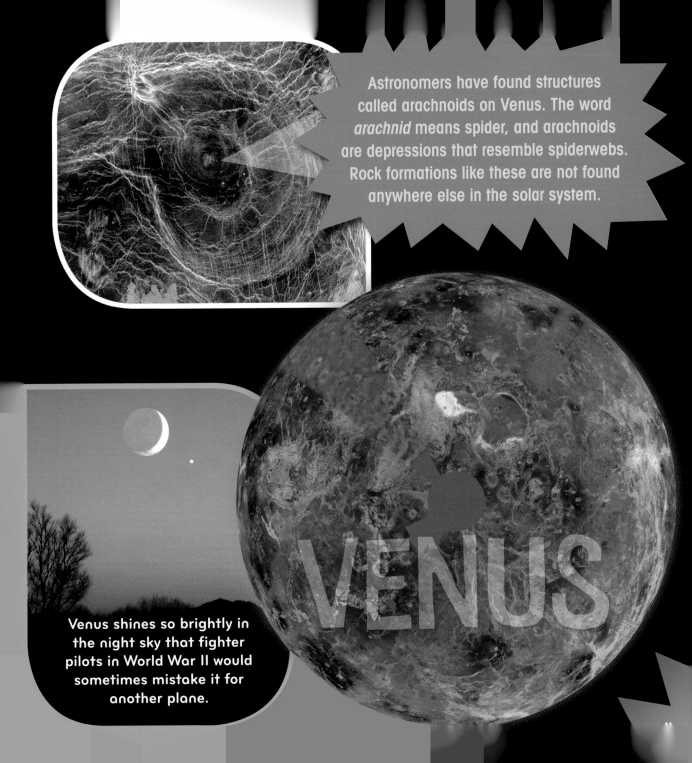

Astronomers have found structures called arachnoids on Venus. The word *arachnid* means spider, and arachnoids are depressions that resemble spiderwebs. Rock formations like these are not found anywhere else in the solar system.

Venus shines so brightly in the night sky that fighter pilots in World War II would sometimes mistake it for another plane.

VENUS

THE MOON

Just as Earth orbits the sun, the moon orbits Earth. Our moon has no atmosphere to shield it from asteroids, rocks, dust, and fast-moving space junk. This same space junk has been crashing into the surface of the moon for billions of years, sometimes traveling 100,000 miles per hour. This is why the surface of the moon looks a lot like Swiss cheese.

The largest crater on the moon is called the South Pole-Aitken Basin and is 1,398 miles across. That means it's about the same size as the entire European Union!

We know the moon once had active volcanoes because the dark areas are filled with basalt, a volcanic rock.

The far side of the moon is covered with impact craters.

When we look at the moon from Earth, we always see the same side. Until Lunar 3 sent back photos in 1959, no one knew what the other side looked like.

Surface of the moon

On the last three Apollo missions, astronauts drove lunar rovers on the moon.

See how tiny this astronaut is compared to a boulder on the moon.

GALAXIES EATING GALAXIES!

Gravity is a powerful, invisible force. Every object in the universe has a gravitational pull. The bigger something is, the more pull, or gravity, it has.

There are galaxies with a gravitational pull so enormous that they swallow all of their neighbors. These "cannibal galaxies" eat everything around them, from stars and planets to smaller galaxies. They then use the materials they "eat" to make new stars and planets.

The average galaxy contains 40 billion stars.

See how bright that galaxy is? Scientists think this galaxy, ESO 306-17, doesn't have any neighboring galaxies because it has gobbled them all up!

These merging galaxies look like glowing eyes.

Here are a few galaxies that are *slowly* colliding and merging.

Four galaxies are grouped so closely that they steal stars from one another and change shape often. This tug-of-war will probably last for billions of years.

The Antennae Galaxies are two spiral galaxies colliding into one another. The glowing blue and pink areas show where billions of new stars are being born.

PLANETARY NEBULAE

A planetary nebula is not a planet or even related to planets. It's a colorful cloud of gas and dust in space. A nebula usually results from the death of a star, and it may be a region where new stars are formed. The plural of *nebula* is *nebulae* (*neb*-yuh-lie).

The Eskimo Nebula was discovered in 1787 by astronomer William Herschel.

Nebulae come in all different shapes and sizes. Some of them have pretty cool names, too.

New stars are being born in this section of the Carina Nebula.

The Bow Tie Nebula was formed with the stuff left over from a dying sun-like star.

The Crab Nebula is the result of an exploding star, or supernova, first observed in 1054.

COMETS

Comets are made up of rocks, dust, and ice from the edge of our solar system. This area, located far out in space—past Pluto—is called the Kuiper Belt. It is insanely cold there.

Comets travel such long distances that it can take anywhere from a few dozen years to many thousands of years for them to travel around the sun. As a comet gets closer to the sun and begins to melt, pieces of rock and dust are released. These chunks of rocks and dust make up the comet's tail. Most comets melt completely when they get close to the sun.

It is very rare that a comet can be seen in the sky without a telescope. Halley's comet and Hale-Bopp are two of the biggest, brightest, and most famous comets. Halley's comet orbits the sun approximately every 76 years.

Comets are usually between a few miles and several hundred miles in length, but their tails can be millions of miles long.

Comet Hale-Bopp was seen
streaming over the Cascade
Mountains in Oregon.

A comet's tail always points
away from the sun.

Comets are sometimes called
"dirty snowballs" because they're
mostly made of ice and dust.

SHOOTING STARS

Have you ever seen a bright light streaking across the night sky? Most people know these as shooting stars. But guess what? They are not stars at all. They are pieces of rock or metal from comets, asteroids, or planets that have entered our atmosphere, and they are called meteors.

When Earth passes through the trail of a comet, the evening sky can light up with the debris from the comet's tail. This is known as a meteor shower.

A meteor falling through space

The Hoba meteorite is the largest meteorite found in one piece. It weighs 66 tons, and was discovered in Namibia, Africa, in 1920.

The atmosphere that surrounds Earth helps to protect the planet from the rocks and debris flying around in space. Because of our atmosphere, most meteors burn up before they ever reach Earth's surface. The ones that hit the ground are called meteorites. When a meteorite hits the ground, it usually leaves a big dent, or crater.

Some meteors slam into the moon so hard that the moon shakes. In 1969, Buzz Aldrin used a seismometer to measure vibrations and "moonquakes."

ASTEROIDS

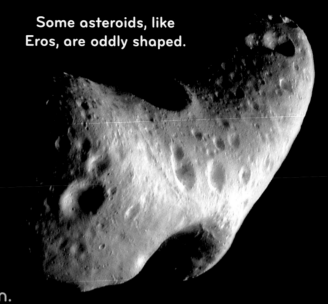

Asteroids are rocky
mini-planets, sometimes
referred to as minor
planets or planetoids.
Most asteroids are found
in the main asteroid
belt, between Mars and
Jupiter. Others, known as
"wandering asteroids," have
their own orbit around the sun.
Trojans are asteroids that follow the
same orbit as Jupiter. Astronomers believe
that Neptune may also have its own collection
of asteroids.

    If an asteroid bumps into something large,
it can get knocked out of its orbit and crash into
a planet or moon.

Asteroid Ida 243 has its
own mini-moon, Dactyl.

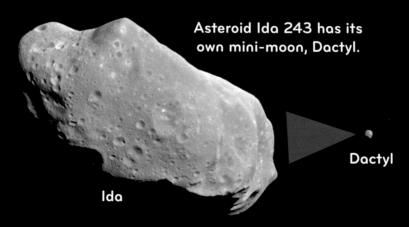

Dactyl

Ida

22

Many asteroids are too small to be seen even with a telescope. But more than 200 asteroids in the asteroid belt are larger than 60 miles across.

Ceres used to be considered the largest known asteroid, at 580 miles across. But, in 2006, Ceres was reclassified as a dwarf planet, making it the only dwarf planet in the asteroid belt.

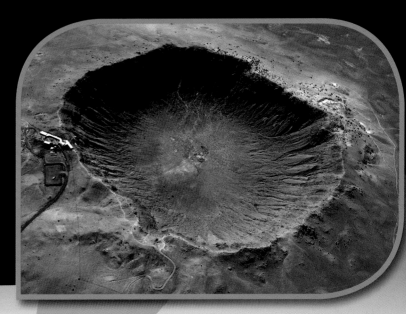

The Barringer Crater in Arizona is thought to be the result of an asteroid hitting Earth about 50,000 years ago.

SATELLITES

If you ever spot a *really* slow-moving shooting star, you probably aren't looking at a star or a meteor. It's probably a man-made satellite!

Satellites help with so many aspects of our lives that most people use them every day. Some satellites are used to connect cell-phone calls or provide Internet access. Others beam TV and radio shows around the world or provide the information for GPS devices. Satellites track weather patterns and look into deep space. Some governments use satellites for high-tech spying.

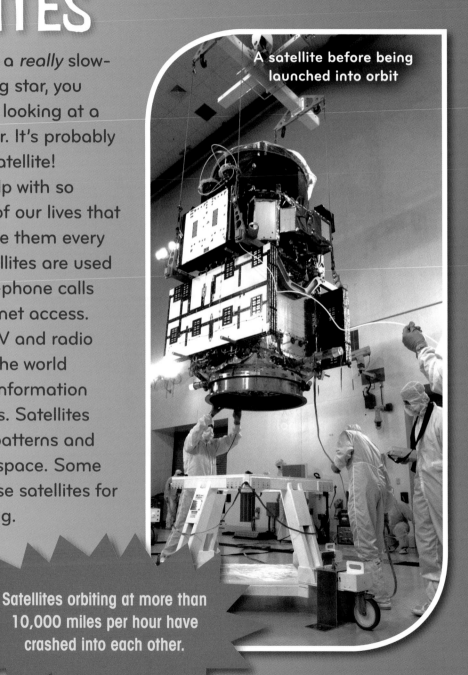

A satellite before being launched into orbit

Satellites orbiting at more than 10,000 miles per hour have crashed into each other.

24

This 590-pound satellite tracks whales off the coast of Argentina.

A small satellite, Starshine 2, is released from the space shuttle *Endeavour* in 2009. Students from 660 schools in 26 countries studied data collected by the satellite. Some even helped polish the 845 mirrors used on the disco ball look-alike!

ONE HIGH-FLYING CAMERA

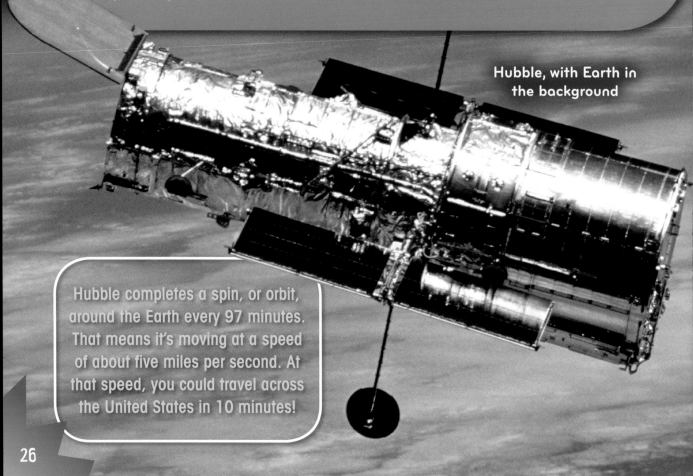

NASA launched the Hubble Space Telescope on April 24, 1990, and it has been orbiting outside Earth's atmosphere ever since. Hubble takes pictures of places that scientists could only dream of before. It has sent hundreds of thousands of images back to Earth. Scientists from around the world take turns using the telescope to explore space and conduct research.

Hubble, with Earth in the background

Hubble completes a spin, or orbit, around the Earth every 97 minutes. That means it's moving at a speed of about five miles per second. At that speed, you could travel across the United States in 10 minutes!

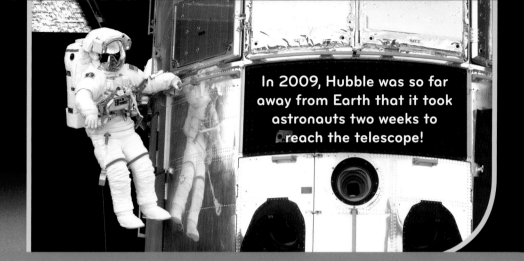

In 2009, Hubble was so far away from Earth that it took astronauts two weeks to reach the telescope!

In 2009, seven astronauts went to Hubble to make repairs. It was a dangerous mission. If the astronauts had not been successful, Hubble would never have sent another image to Earth.

Hubble is expected to continue snapping pictures until at least 2013. Once it is no longer operational and starts to fall out of orbit, a robot is expected to guide Hubble through the atmosphere and into the ocean.

Astronauts trained for the Hubble repair mission by working inside a huge water tank.

A SNEAK PEEK INTO
DEEP SPACE

The photographs taken by Hubble are extra special because they allow us to see farther into space than ever before.

This is the center of the Whirlpool Galaxy, which is about 31 million light-years away from the Milky Way Galaxy, where we live. Hubble captured this photo in 2001.

Earth's atmosphere protects us from harmful radiation and from any rocks or debris that may fall to Earth from space. It also filters out certain wavelengths of light that tell scientists a great deal about the universe. To look deep into space, scientists had to place the Hubble telescope outside of our atmosphere.

This rose-shaped galaxy is made up of two spiral galaxies playing tug-of-war with each other.

Here are a few of Hubble's best shots.

Hubble photographed this gas cloud, or nebula, 650 light-years away. The amazing colors look like an eye in the sky!

These beautiful columns of hydrogen gas and dust are the birthplace of stars inside the Eagle Nebula.

ANIMALS IN SPACE

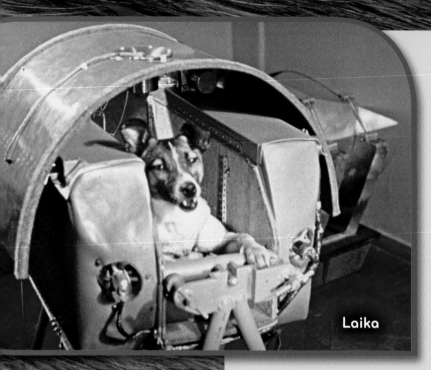

Laika

Before sending a person into orbit, scientists sent animals into space to make sure it was safe.

The first animal launched into orbit was the Soviet dog Laika, in November 1957. Unfortunately, Laika survived only the first five to seven hours of the four-day flight.

Many more dogs flew to space, and scientists studied how their bodies were affected by space travel. A few pups came back constipated (which means they had trouble going number two). This is how scientists discovered that anyone going into space would need a high-fiber diet (because more fiber means easier pooping).

Just like human astronauts, dogs had to train to sit in tiny spaces for hours, to use weird bathroom contraptions, and to eat odd, gooey space food.

A few years after Laika, in 1960, two Soviet dogs, Strelka and Belka, launched into orbit aboard Sputnik 5. The dogs were accompanied by a gray rabbit, 42 mice, two rats, some flies, and different kinds of plants and fungi. They became the first creatures to successfully orbit the Earth. All the animals and plants on board returned to Earth safely.

Model of Sputnik 5

An astronaut aboard a space shuttle, in 1994, examines a newt that came along for the ride.

FTOFF

Takeoff and landing are the most complicated and dangerous aspects of spaceflight. Two space shuttles and their crews have been lost during this process. *Challenger* exploded about one minute into its launch in 1986, and *Columbia* broke apart while reentering the Earth's atmosphere in 2003. *Columbia* was traveling 12,500 miles per hour at the time.

Sally Ride

Sally Ride, the first American woman in space, described what liftoff is like. "When you're getting ready to launch into space, you're sitting on a big explosion waiting to happen. . . . It's very different from any experience you can have on Earth. . . . . we practice in simulators, it's not the same—it's not even close to the same. It's a very exciting experience."

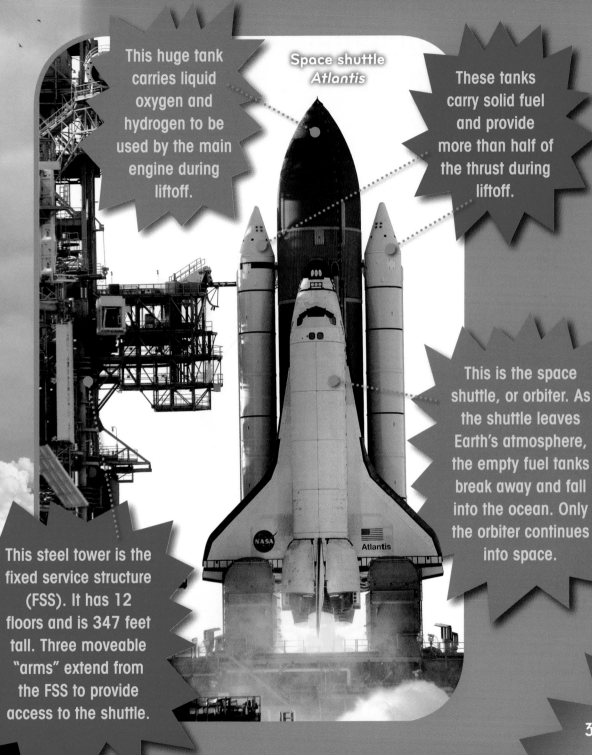

This huge tank carries liquid oxygen and hydrogen to be used by the main engine during liftoff.

Space shuttle *Atlantis*

These tanks carry solid fuel and provide more than half of the thrust during liftoff.

This is the space shuttle, or orbiter. As the shuttle leaves Earth's atmosphere, the empty fuel tanks break away and fall into the ocean. Only the orbiter continues into space.

This steel tower is the fixed service structure (FSS). It has 12 floors and is 347 feet tall. Three moveable "arms" extend from the FSS to provide access to the shuttle.

NASA

Atlantis

THE INTERNATIONAL SPACE STATION

The International Space Station (ISS) might just be the coolest research station in the solar system. It orbits Earth about 220 miles above the planet, moving at about five miles per second. The first part of the ISS was launched in November 1998, and astronauts added more pieces over the next two years. In October 2000, the first crew members arrived. Since then, nearly 200 people from eight countries have lived and worked on the ISS.

The ISS has about as much living space as a five-bedroom home. There are two bathrooms and a gymnasium there!

This is an unpiloted ISS supply spacecraft. It is delivering more than 2.5 tons of fuel, food, oxygen, and supplies to the ISS.

End to end, the International Space Station is almost as long as a football field.

Astronauts in space love their fresh fruit deliveries!

LIVING ON A SPACE STATION

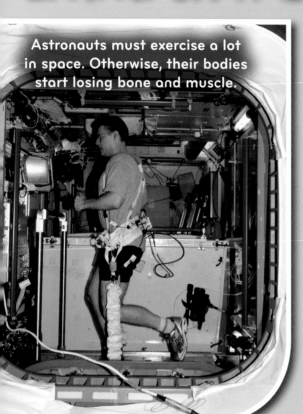

Astronauts must exercise a lot in space. Otherwise, their bodies start losing bone and muscle.

Without the pull of Earth's gravity, astronauts float. Weightlessness sounds fun, but it also confuses your brain and body. The result is space adaptation syndrome, or what one astronaut described as "a fancy term for throwing up." More than half of all space travelers suffer from space sickness, with headaches, poor concentration, nausea, and vomiting.

The good news is that you may stop snoring in space because gravity is an important factor in snoring! Of course, the sun rises and sets every 90 minutes in low Earth orbit, making it really hard to sleep well on the ISS.

Valeri Polyakov holds the record for the longest space mission. He spent 438 days aboard Mir, the Russian space station, in 1994–95.

Greg Chamitoff plays a far-out game of chess with Mission Control on Earth.

Hair trimmers are connected to vacuums so the cut pieces don't fly all over the cabin and clog up machinery.

Astronauts zip into their sleeping bags so they don't float away while they sleep.

Crew members celebrate holidays in space.

Astronaut Cady Coleman brought her flutes on her mission.

SPACE FOOD

Early NASA astronauts were stuck with a very limited menu. Bite-size cubes of dried food; chalky, freeze-dried powders; and semi-liquids squeezed out of aluminum tubes were all they ate for days on end. Seriously, toothpaste food? Yuck. It was no surprise that astronauts complained.

Apollo astronauts were the first to have hot water, which made rehydrating foods easier—and tastier.

Water had to be added to this 1965 packet of beef pot roast before it was ready to eat.

A lot of the foods that astronauts now eat are just like the ones in your grocery store.

In 1965, John Young smuggled a corned beef sandwich onto *Gemini 3* as a gag gift for his fellow astronaut, Gus Grissom. Two hours into the flight, he pulled out the sandwich, and it began to break apart immediately. Young got in tons of trouble.

Over the years, better packaging improved food quality and selection. At the beginning of each mission, they even have fresh fruit.

Astronauts use salt and pepper only in liquid form. This is because sprinkling is tricky in zero gravity. Grains of salt and pepper floating into equipment or an astronaut's eyes or nose could be a real problem.

In zero gravity, drops of water can float away!

Space food is vacuum-sealed into packages with Velcro on the back.

Candy-coated chocolate and candy-coated peanuts are many astronauts' favorite snacks.

Macaroni and cheese

39

ROBOTS TO THE RESCUE!

Space travel is dangerous, and it takes a serious toll on an astronaut's body. Humans may become sick due to radiation, or bone or muscle loss. Robots, however, never get sick. They don't need air, food, water, or rest. And they don't get tired or bored doing the exact same task over and over. Space agencies have been using robots for years, but now scientists are developing more advanced, humanoid robots or Robonauts.

A space shuttle *Atlantis* astronaut is attached to a robotic arm by a foot strap. The robotic arm helps astronauts move equipment and perform repairs.

These robots are known as Robonauts 2. They are able to use the same tools as humans.

Robonaut 2 (or R2, for short) can be mounted atop a wheeled base. This will allow the robot to explore the surfaces of far-off planets.

Astronaut Scott Kelly and a Robonaut 2 pose aboard the ISS.

41

ROBO-SCIENTISTS ON MARS

SPIRIT ROVER

This **antenna** is used to trade information with a spacecraft orbiting Mars.

Panoramic cameras allow the rover to take huge, wide photos of their surroundings.

This **antenna** is used for communicating with Earth.

Solar cells collect energy that is used to power the robot's batteries.

A **microscopic imager** takes extra close-up photos.

This is called a **rock abrasion tool.** It grinds into rocks and collects dust and rock pieces.

This is an **alpha particle X-ray spectrometer (APWS).** It collects information that helps scientists figure out what Mars rocks and soil are made of.

Cameras mounted here help the rover to avoid rocks and other hazards.

Geologists are scientists who study rocks and minerals. The Mars Exploration Rovers are robot geologists! These robots have cameras, microscopes, rock grinders, magnets, and solar panels to help them collect and share information about Mars.

NASA landed Mars rovers *Spirit* and *Opportunity* on two separate areas of Mars in 2004. For more than six years, *Spirit* roamed Mars, covering nearly 5 miles and returning more than 124,000 images. *Opportunity* rover is still going strong.

Mars is often called the Red Planet because the rust in the rock there makes it glow an orangey-red color.

The *Pathfinder* rover snapped this shot of *Sojourner* and Mars's rocky surface in 1997.

A new rover, *Curiosity*, is set to launch in late 2011.

WOULD YOU MAKE A GREAT ASTRONAUT?

Do you like science and math? Have you ever wanted to be a pilot? Do you love to travel? These are just a few of the interests that could help prepare you for a trip out of this world.

Becoming an astronaut takes years of study and training. The best astronauts are disciplined, hard workers, and they always keep cool under pressure. Because they have to live in tiny spaces with their fellow space travelers, they also have to be team players. Astronauts need to be able to sleep while floating and be willing to eat weird food.

The average age of an astronaut is 34.

China's space agency does not accept astronauts who have bad breath. Nobody wants to be stuck in a tiny space capsule with a stinky shipmate!

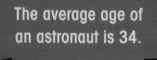

IF YOU WANT TO BE AN ASTRONAUT, HERE ARE A FEW THINGS YOU CAN DO:

Stay in shape. Eat lots of fruits and vegetables, and get plenty of exercise.

Practice in the pool. You'll need to be a good swimmer for astronaut training.

Study hard. Get good grades and learn all you can about science, space, engineering, or computers.

Try a team sport.

Go on planes, trains, boats, and amusement-park rides. If you get motion sickness and barf a lot, then space travel probably isn't for you.

Learn another language. Speaking Russian or Japanese will help you communicate with the astronauts aboard the ISS.

Astronaut Leland Melvin says, "You can't win a game if you can't work with your team. Working in the tight spaces of the shuttle or the [space] station takes teamwork as well."

SPACE TECHNOLOGY ON EARTH

Many people think the space program has no direct effect on their lives, but this couldn't be farther from the truth. The things that space scientists and engineers have learned have been used to improve computer processors, compact discs (CDs), water-purification systems, flat-panel television screens, electric cars, helmets, ski goggles, batteries, and countless medical technologies.

The dents on a golf ball are called dimples. To find out what dimple pattern makes for the fastest-flying golf balls, ball makers used NASA's super-high speed cameras to see how golf balls spin when hit.

Scientists looked into using algae to help with recycling on long flights. They ended up creating an algae-based substance with lots of nutrients that's now used in baby food!

Scratch-resistant eyeglass lenses are coated with a substance that was originally developed for astronauts' helmets.

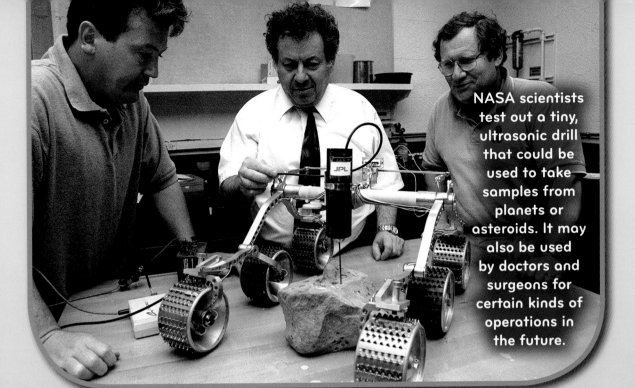

NASA scientists test out a tiny, ultrasonic drill that could be used to take samples from planets or asteroids. It may also be used by doctors and surgeons for certain kinds of operations in the future.

When designers wanted to make swimsuits that wouldn't slow down swimmers—not even a fraction of a second—they went to the space experts. Most Olympic swimmers now wear bathing suits developed with these findings.

Running shoes use technology from moon boots to increase stability and improve shock absorption.

47

SPACE ROCKS ON EARTH: TEKTITES

In 1968, a scientist displays some tektites found in Thailand.

The rocks that come with this book are called tektites. Many scientists believe they were formed when meteorites crashed into Earth. The extreme speed, heat, and impact of the meteorites melted whatever they landed on. The material then hardened into tektites.

Scientists think the melted meteorite and bits of Earth were hurled back into the air after impact and scattered about. The rock and debris may have hardened mid-flight, which might explain why some are shaped like teardrops or dumbbells.

Tektites look like glass and have lower water content than any other rocks on Earth. These unusual stones come in many shapes and sizes. What shapes are your tektites?

The large areas where tektites are found are called "strewnfields."